Pet Corner / Rincón de las mascotas

TERRIFIC TURTLES/ TORTUGAS ASOMBROSAS

By Rose Carraway

Traducción al español: Eduardo Alamán

Gareth Stevens Publishing

Please visit our website, www.garethstevens.com. For a free color catalog of all our high-quality books, call toll free 1-800-542-2595 or fax 1-877-542-2596.

Library of Congress Cataloging-in-Publication Data

Carraway, Rose.
[Terrific turtles. Spanish & English]
Terrific turtles = Tortugas asombrosas / Rose Carraway.
p. cm. — (Pet corner = Rincón de las mascotas)
Includes index.
ISBN 978-1-4339-6647-7 (library binding)
1. Turtles as pets—Juvenile literature. I. Title.
SF459.T8C36618 2012
639.3'92—dc23

2011026958

First Edition

Published in 2012 by
Gareth Stevens Publishing
111 East 14th Street, Suite 349
New York, NY 10003

Editor: Katie Kawa
Designer: Andrea Davison-Bartolotta
Spanish Translation: Eduardo Alamán

Photo credits: Cover, pp. 1, 7, 9, 11, 15, 19, 21 (food), 23, 24 (shell) Shutterstock.com; pp. 5, 21 (main) iStockphoto/Thinkstock; pp. 13, 24 (pen) iStockphoto.com; pp. 17, 24 (tank) ballyscanlon/Photonica/Getty Images.

Printed in the United States of America

CPSIA compliance information: Batch #CW12GS: For further information contact Gareth Stevens, New York, New York at 1-800-542-2595.

Contents

Contenido

Turtles make cool pets!

¡Las tortugas son buenas mascotas!

A turtle can hide
in its shell.

Las tortugas se
esconden en su
caparazón.

Its head, legs, and feet go inside.

La cabeza, piernas y pies se meten en el caparazón.

One kind of pet turtle
is an aquatic turtle.
It lives in water.

Una clase de tortuga
es la tortuga acuática.
La tortuga acuática
vive en el agua.

Some pet turtles
live outside.
They live in a pen.

Algunas tortugas
mascota viven al aire
libre. Viven en un corral.

They sleep all winter.
This is called hibernating.

Las tortugas duermen durante el invierno.
A esto se le llama invernar.

Some pet turtles
live inside.
They live in glass tanks.

Algunas tortugas
mascota viven dentro
de las casas. Viven en
tanques de vidrio.

Turtles eat many things. They like fish.

Las tortugas comen muchas cosas. A las tortugas les gusta el pescado.

They eat sticks
of turtle food, too.

Además, comen
"pellets" de comida
para tortuga.

Turtles can live
for a long time.
Some are 100 years old!

Las tortugas viven mucho
tiempo. ¡Algunas viven
hasta 100 años!

Words to Know/ Palabras que debes saber

pen/
(el) corral

shell/
(el) caparazón

tank/
(el) tanque

Index / Índice